SAMSUNG GALAXY S20,

S20 PLUS, S20 ULTRA

WELL-DETAILED USER'S GUIDE

Fast and Easy Approach to get over the usage of Samsung
Galaxy S20 series and its handy tips and tricks

MICHAEL

JOSH

Copyright

Printed in the United States of America

© 2019 by Michael Josh

Churchgate Publishing House

USA | UK | Canada

Table of Contents

Why This Guide?

To start with, congratulations on getting the new Samsung s20, s20 plus, s20 ultra. Samsung company has been producing magnificent phones as far back their existence. Fast forward to this writing. This user guide is pointing at, the Samsung galaxy s20 series, which is the beast among Samsung phones as of this writing. What makes this phone unique among all is that it was built on upgraded hardware, which enhances its premium features and some hidden tricks and tips.

To get the best out of this device, this user guide will give you insights and help on how to go about handling the hidden features, numerous handy tips, and tricks of the Samsung galaxy s20 series.

About the Author

 Michael josh is a tech explorer with over 12 years of experience in the ICT sector. He developed himself with his advancement in the field of information communication technology, which facilitates his writing skills. His hobby is exploring new things and fixing problems in its most straightforward form has been his focus ever since. Michael obtained a Bachelor's and a Master's Degree in Computer Science and Information Communication Technology from New Jersey Institute of Technology Newark, NJ.

Chapter 1

Evolution of Samsung Galaxy S series

To commend how far Samsung S series has developed over the years, we will brush on coming into existence of Samsung Galaxy S series starting from the first (Samsung galaxy S) which was introduced to the populace back in march 2010 to the Samsung galaxy s20 ultra that was launched February 11, 2020. The Samsung galaxy s20 series is the latest S series as of the writing of this book.

Samsung Galaxy (S, S+)

The launch of Samsung Galaxy S quite brings about the success of the company. In three years, Samsung sold 25million Galaxy S units, which influence the manufacturer to release a successor in no time. During this time, Samsung produces sub-variant of S, which is known as S+ before the release of its successor.

Samsung Galaxy S
Released March, 2010

ANDROID 2.1 | HUMMINGBIRD | AMOLED DISPLAY

DISPLAY **4"**

CAMERAS **5MP** FRONT VGA

INTERNAL STORAGE **8/16GB** UP TO 16GB

RAM **512MB**

BATTERY **1500** mAh

WEIGHT **119g**

Samsung Galaxy S Plus
Released April, 2011

ANDROID 2.3 | SNAPDRAGON S2 | AMOLED DISPLAY

DISPLAY **4"**

CAMERAS **5MP** FRONT VGA

INTERNAL STORAGE **8/16GB** UP TO 16GB

RAM **512MB**

BATTERY **1650** mAh

WEIGHT **119g**

The Galaxy S featured a physical home key below its display and a capacitive key on each side. It has a 4-inch display, which was considered large at the time. The galaxy s was built on Samsung Exynos 3110 CPU, a single processor, and it runs Android 2.1 (Eclair), which is upgradeable to 2.3 (Gingerbread). The phone includes 512MB RAM and 8/16GB ROM. A detachable battery

4

🔋 of 1500mah capacity, body made of plastic and a back VGA camera 📷

Samsung Galaxy s2

The Samsung Galaxy s2 was announced a year after its predecessor in February 2011. Even though the phone was made out of polycarbonate (plastic), nevertheless, there is an improvement to the body design over Samsung Galaxy S and S plus.

Samsung Galaxy S2 Plus

Released January, 2013

DISPLAY 4.3"

CAMERAS 8MP FRONT 2MP

INTERNAL STORAGE 8GB UP TO 16GB

RAM 1GB

BATTERY 1650 mAh

WEIGHT 121g

The phone utilizes a removable back cover with a removable 1,650mah capacity battery as the first generation. The physical home key made a re-occur along with the two capacitive buttons, and the galaxy s2 offers an improvement in the camera with an 8-megapixel primary sensor. The device came with improved display compared to the Galaxy S and S plus as it included a 4.3-inch super AMOLED panel. The phone was built on Exynos 4210 dual, Snapdragons3, and TI OMAP 4430 (depends on the buyer's choice), and this was coupled with android 2.3 (gingerbread) with 4.1 (jelly bean) OTA update made available for it as the last update. The company managed to sold 3 million phones in less than two months after the galaxy s2 was launched. The phone was also a success for the company as it sold 40 million units Samsung galaxy s2 at the end. It also has sub-variant, which is called s2+, with a few differences in their specifications. Check the image above.

Samsung Galaxy s3

On may 2012, the Samsung galaxy s3 was announced by its manufacturer. It was an improved version of s2 and s2+. The Galaxy s3 featured a 4.8-inch HD super AMOLED display, 1GB RAM, and three storage variants available. The processor was Exynos 4412 Quad, and Snapdragon s4 (depending on the buyer's choice) with an 8-megapixel camera included on the back.

Samsung Galaxy S3
Released May, 2012

ANDROID 4.0.4   EXYNOS 4412   AMOLED DISPLAY

DISPLAY **4.8"**   CAMERAS **8MP** FRONT 1.9MP

INTERNAL STORAGE **16/32GB** UP TO 16GB   RAM **1GB**

BATTERY **2100** mAh   WEIGHT **133g**

Samsung Galaxy S3 Mini

Released October, 2012

ANDROID 4.1	NOVA THOR U8420	AMOLED DISPLAY

 DISPLAY **4"**   **CAMERAS** **5MP** FRONT VGA

INTERNAL STORAGE **8/16GB** UP TO 32GB   **RAM** **1GB**

BATTERY **1500** mAh   **WEIGHT** **111g**

Samsung Galaxy S3 Mini VE

Released October, 2012

ANDROID 4.1.2	NOVA THOR U8420	AMOLED DISPLAY

 DISPLAY **4"**   **CAMERAS** **5MP** FRONT VGA

INTERNAL STORAGE **8/16GB** UP TO 32GB   **RAM** **1GB**

 BATTERY **1500** mAh   **WEIGHT** **120g**

Samsung Galaxy S3 Neo

Released April, 2014

ANDROID 4.3	SNAPDRAGON 400	AMOLED DISPLAY

 DISPLAY **4.8"**   **CAMERAS** **8MP** FRONT 1.9MP

INTERNAL STORAGE **16GB** UP TO 32GB   **RAM** **1.5GB**

 BATTERY **2100** mAh   **WEIGHT** **132g**

8

The phone also featured a physical home key, and one capacitive key on each side with the home key thinner compare to the first two generations and their sub-variants. The android version 4.0.4 (ice cream sandwich) was pre-installed on the phone, and android 4.3 (Jelly Bean) was the last official update made available for the phone. The phone featured a detachable 2100mah capacity battery, and the phone was made out of plastic-like its predecessors, though the back cover was more slippery and look a lot more different to the previous devices. This phone has three sub-variants. The S3 mini, s3 mini VE, and s3 Neo.

Samsung managed to sell an encouraged 70 million galaxy s3 units overall, with 9 million pre-orders having been placed before the phone was released. By this time, the s series was known as the android's flagship series.

Samsung Galaxy s4

The Samsung galaxy s4, which is the fourth series of Samsung galaxy s series, was announced in March 2013, and it almost has the same look with the s3 with few little differences. The ratio of its bezel was small compare to s3 likewise, the body design, which was made out of polycarbonate (plastic). At the same time, the physical home key was located below along two capacitive keys, similar to the galaxy s3.

Samsung Galaxy S4
Released March, 2013

ANDROID 4.2.2 EXYNOS 5410 AMOLED DISPLAY

 DISPLAY
5"

 CAMERAS
13MP
FRONT 2MP

 INTERNAL STORAGE
16/32/64GB
UP TO 32GB

 RAM
2GB

 BATTERY
2600 mAh

 WEIGHT
130g

Samsung Galaxy S4 Mini
Released May, 2013

ANDROID 4.2.2 SNAPDRAGON 400 AMOLED DISPLAY

 DISPLAY
4.3"

CAMERAS
8MP
FRONT 1.9MP

 INTERNAL STORAGE
8GB
UP TO 32GB

 RAM
1.5GB

 BATTERY
1900 mAh

 WEIGHT
107g

10

Samsung Galaxy S4 Active
Released June. 2013

ANDROID 4.2.2 • SNAPDRAGON 600 • TFT DISPLAY • IP67 CERTIFICATION

DISPLAY 5"

CAMERAS 8MP FRONT 2MP

INTERNAL STORAGE 16GB UP TO 32GB

RAM 2GB

BATTERY 2600 mAh

WEIGHT 153g

Samsung Galaxy S4 Zoom
Released June. 2013

ANDROID 4.2.2 • MEGA DUAL 1.5GHz • AMOLED DISPLAY

DISPLAY 4.3"

CAMERAS 16MP FRONT 1.9MP

INTERNAL STORAGE 8GB UP TO 32GB

RAM 1.5GB

BATTERY 2330 mAh

WEIGHT 208g

The galaxy s4 has a large display than the s3, as it arrived with a 5.0-inch full Hd super AMOLED display, and the device was built on Exynos 5410 octa/Snapdragon 600 though, a special LTE variant that was launched later had snapdragon 800 CPU.

The phone came with a 13-megapixel on the back and a removable battery of 2600mah capacity. The phone came with android version 4.2.2 (Jelly Bean), and the last official update received was android version 5.0.1 (lollipop).

In the first four days, the manufacturer managed to sell 4 million Galaxy s4 units, and in 27 days, 10 million was sold. In six months, 40 million Galaxy s4 units were sold. Samsung Galaxy s4 has three sub-variants, check the image above.

Samsung Galaxy s5

The Samsung Galaxy s5 was still made out of polycarbonate (plastic). It also came with a very similar physical home key, two capacitive keys to the Galaxy s3 and s4.

This device was announced in February 2014 with a display of 5.1-inch full-HD super AMOLED, and it was the very first Samsung Galaxy S series to offer water and dust resistance. The Galaxy s5 was built on Snapdragon 801/Exynos 5 octa 5422 SoC with a special LTE-A variant that came with snapdragon 805 SoC.

Samsung Galaxy S5
Released February, 2014

ANDROID 4.4.2   SNAPDRAGON 801   AMOLED DISPLAY   FINGERPRINT   IP67 CERTIFICATION

DISPLAY **5.1"**

CAMERAS **16MP** FRONT 2MP

INTERNAL STORAGE **16/32GB** UP TO 64GB

RAM **2GB**

BATTERY **2800** mAh

WEIGHT **145g**

Samsung Galaxy S5 Mini

Released June, 2014

ANDROID 4.4.2   EXYNOS 3470   AMOLED DISPLAY   FINGERPRINT   IP67 CERTIFICATION

 DISPLAY **4.5"**   **CAMERAS** **8MP** FRONT 2.1MP

 INTERNAL STORAGE **16GB** UP TO 32GB   **RAM** **1.5GB**

 BATTERY **2100 mAh**   **WEIGHT** **120g**

Samsung Galaxy S5 Plus

Released October, 2014

ANDROID 4.4.2   SNAPDRAGON 805   AMOLED DISPLAY   FINGERPRINT   IP67 CERTIFICATION

 DISPLAY **5.1"**   **CAMERAS** **16MP** FRONT 2MP

 INTERNAL STORAGE **16/32GB** UP TO 64GB   **RAM** **2GB**

 BATTERY **2800 mAh**   **WEIGHT** **145g**

Samsung Galaxy S5 Sport

Released June, 2014

ANDROID 4.4.2   SNAPDRAGON 801   AMOLED DISPLAY   IP68 CERTIFICATION

 DISPLAY **5.1"**   **CAMERAS** **16MP** FRONT 2MP

 INTERNAL STORAGE **16GB** UP TO 64GB   **RAM** **2GB**

 BATTERY **2800 mAh**   **WEIGHT** **158g**

Samsung Galaxy S5 Active
Released May, 2014

ANDROID 4.4.2 · SNAPDRAGON 801 · AMOLED DISPLAY · IP67 CERTIFICATION

DISPLAY **5.1"** · CAMERAS **16MP** FRONT 2MP

INTERNAL STORAGE **16GB** UP TO 32GB · RAM **2GB**

BATTERY **2800** mAh · WEIGHT **170g**

This device included 2GB RAM and 16/32GB ROM (expandable) with a detachable 2800mah capacity battery. This show to be the last galaxy s series to feature a removable battery. Android version 4.4.4 (KitKat) was pre-installed, and the last official update was Android 6, which is known as MARSHMALLOW.

This device was also the first galaxy S series to offer a fingerprint scanner with the fingerprint embedded in the physical home key and the capacitive keys on both sides.

In the first three months of sales, Samsung sold 12 million Galaxy s5.

Samsung Galaxy s6

This series has two sub-variants the s6 EDGE and s6 EDGE+. On March 6, the s6 and s6 EDGE was announced while the 6 EDGE+ was announced in August.

Samsung Galaxy S6 Edge
Released March, 2015

 ANDROID 5.0.2   EXYNOS 7420   AMOLED DISPLAY   FINGERPRINT

DISPLAY
5.1"

CAMERAS
16MP
FRONT 5MP

INTERNAL STORAGE
32/64/128GB
NO CARD SLOT

RAM
3GB

BATTERY
2600 mAh
FAST CHARGE 15W

WEIGHT
132g

Samsung Galaxy S6 Edge+
Released August, 2015

ANDROID 5.1.1   EXYNOS 7420   AMOLED DISPLAY   FINGERPRINT

DISPLAY
5.7"

CAMERAS
16MP
FRONT 5MP

INTERNAL STORAGE
32/64/128GB
NO CARD SLOT

RAM
4GB

BATTERY
3000 mAh
FAST CHARGE 15W

WEIGHT
153g

  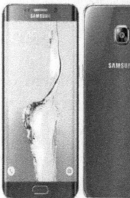 

Samsung Galaxy S6
Released March, 2015

ANDROID 5.0.2   EXYNOS 7420   AMOLED DISPLAY   FINGERPRINT

DISPLAY
5.1"

CAMERAS
16MP
FRONT 5MP

INTERNAL STORAGE
32/64/128GB
NO CARD SLOT

RAM
3GB

BATTERY
2550 mAh
FAST CHARGE 15W

WEIGHT
138g

15

The galaxy s6 EDGE+ has distinct specs as it included aa 5.7-inch QHD+ Super AMOLED curved display with 4GB RAM and an improved battery capacity of 3000 mah compared to the 2600mah provided for s6 EDGE.

The phone came with Android version 5.0.2 lollipop, and all the galaxy s6 models were eventually updated to Android 8.0 Oreo, which was the last official update for the galaxy s6 series.

Within one month of release, Samsung sold 10 million galaxies s6 series and overall, 45 million units in total.

Samsung Galaxy s7

Samsung launched two phones, the s7 and s7 EDGE, but s7 EDGE+ was pend. Samsung launched the first two in February 2016. As there was a slight difference in the variants of s6 series, the same thing is applicable here. The s7 was fueled with a 5.1-inch QHD Super AMOLED display and the s7 EDGE with a 5.4-inch QHD super AMOLED display with a curved display. The phone was made in two countries, different versions, and there is one of the USA which featured Snapdragon 820 while the European version featured Exynos 8890.

Samsung Galaxy S7 Edge
Released February, 2016

ANDROID 6.0 · EXYNOS 8890 · AMOLED DISPLAY · FINGERPRINT · IP68 CERTIFICATION

DISPLAY
5.5"

CAMERAS
12MP
FRONT 5MP

INTERNAL STORAGE
32/64/128GB
UP TO 128GB

RAM
4GB

BATTERY
3600 mAh
FAST CHARGE 15W

WEIGHT
157g

Samsung Galaxy S7
Released February, 2016

ANDROID 6.0 · EXYNOS 8890 · AMOLED DISPLAY · FINGERPRINT · IP68 CERTIFICATION

DISPLAY
5.1"

CAMERAS
12MP
FRONT 5MP

INTERNAL STORAGE
32/64GB
UP TO 128GB

RAM
4GB

BATTERY
3000 mAh
FAST CHARGE 15W

WEIGHT
152g

The Samsung s7 and s7 EDGE included 4GB of RAM and internal storage of different variants. A single 12-megapixel camera on the back and physical home key embedded with fingerprint with capacitive keys on both sides. It happened to be the last S series with this setup.

These two phones were first s series to offer wireless charging. The phone was pre-installed with android version 6.0 (Marshmallow), and 8.0 (Oreo) was the last official update for both phones.

17

The sales of the phone were much as Samsung sold a total of 48 million units in 2016.

Samsung Galaxy s8

S8 was a vast improvement to its predecessors from design to screen size back to fingerprint position, then camera quality and processor. It represented an entire change to the series and was launched on March 12, 2017. It is probably the biggest change-up till this moment as of the writing of this book.

Samsung Galaxy S8
Released March, 2017

ANDROID 7.0 | EXYNOS 8895 | AMOLED DISPLAY | IRIS SCANNER | IP68 CERTIFICATION

DISPLAY **5.8"**

CAMERAS **12MP** FRONT 8MP

INTERNAL STORAGE **64GB** UP TO 256GB

RAM **4GB**

BATTERY **3000** mAh FAST CHARGE 15W

WEIGHT **155g**

Samsung Galaxy S8 Plus
Released March, 2017

ANDROID 7.0 | EXYNOS 8895 | AMOLED DISPLAY | IRIS SCANNER | IP68 CERTIFICATION

DISPLAY **6.2"**

CAMERAS **12MP** FRONT 8MP

INTERNAL STORAGE **64/128GB** UP TO 256GB

RAM **4/6GB**

BATTERY **3500** mAh FAST CHARGE 15W

WEIGHT **173g**

The galaxy s8 series were familiar but identical with display size. Both featured curved QHD+ Super AMOLED display, but the galaxy s8 had a 5.8-inch display and s8+ featured 6.2-inches display. Conversely, both came with thinner bezels compared to s7 Series.

Samsung switched from the physical home button to on-screen buttons and changed the position of the fingerprint from front to back.

The European version of the phone came with Exynos 8895, while the USA version fueled Snapdragon 835. Both phones featured a 12-megapixel camera on the back, but the battery was another slight difference. s8 was coupled with 3000mah capacity while s8+ featured with an additional 500mah. Both devices supported wireless charging. The pre-installed Android version was 7.1 (Nougat), and both phones were upgraded to android 8.0 (Oreo).

Both phones were a huge success for the company. The galaxy s8 series sold 30% more compared to the galaxy s7 series during the following release months.

Samsung galaxy s9

The Samsung galaxy s9 series arrived in February 2018 in two forms, galaxy s9, and s9+. These devices were made of glass and metal. These two devices were identical, but the only difference in both is the battery capacity, fingerprint, and camera. Consider their difference specifications; the galaxy s9 features 3000mah battery capacity while s9+ featured 3500mah, galaxy s9 offers a single 12-megapixel camera lens on the back, and the s9+ was shipped with dual rear 12+12-megapixel cameras on the back.

Talking about the s9 modules display, both devices featured curved QHD+ super AMOLED displays, rear-positioned fingerprint scanner, and water and dust resistance. S9 featured 5.8-ich and s9+ featured a 6.2-inch display.

These two phones were powered with Exynos 9810 and Snapdragon 845 (depending on the buyer's choice). The phone came with android version 8.1 Oreo with an option to 9.0 Pie.

Samsung Galaxy s10 series

Samsung marked the tenth anniversary with its galaxy s10 series of smartphones, and for the first time, Samsung introduced four devices out of the bat.

The Samsung galaxy s10 series was launched in February 2019 with the following beasts Galaxy s10e, s10, s10+, and s10 5G. All these looked similar and were built on the same CPU SoC Exynos 9820/ Snapdragon 855 (depending on buyer's choice).

Samsung Galaxy S10 Plus
Released February, 2019

ANDROID 9.0 · EXYNOS 9820 · AMOLED DISPLAY · FINGERPRINT · IP68 CERTIFICATION

DISPLAY **6.4"** QW HD+

CAMERAS **12+16+12MP** FRONT 10+8MP

INTERNAL STORAGE **128/512GB** UP TO 1TB

RAM **8/12GB**

BATTERY **4100** mAh FAST CHARGE 25W

WEIGHT **175g** CERAMIC(198g)

Samsung Galaxy S10e
Released February, 2019

ANDROID 9.0 · EXYNOS 9820 · AMOLED DISPLAY · FINGERPRINT · IP68 CERTIFICATION

DISPLAY **5.8"** FULL HD+

CAMERAS **12+16MP** FRONT 10MP

INTERNAL STORAGE **128/256GB** UP TO 512GB

RAM **6/8GB**

BATTERY **3100** mAh FAST CHARGE 15W

WEIGHT **150g**

The smallest of all among s10 series is the Galaxy s10e, which came with a 5.8-inch full-HD+ Dynamic AMOLED display and side facing fingerprint. It's also only an s10 series with a flat display. It featured 12+16-megapixel on the back and a 10-megapixel in front.

The galaxy s10 and s10+ was an improved version of s10e. They included QHD+ curved dynamic AMOLED displays with 6.1-inch and 6.4-inch, respectively. The s10 featured triple cameras on the back and a punch-hole camera in front with 12+12+16-megapixel and, 10-megapixel respectively. The s10 5G came with quad cameras on the back and double punch hole in the front with 12+12+16-megapixel and 12+8-megapixel, respectively, with a larger display of 6.7-inch display and 5G connectivity.

Samsung Galaxy s20 series

The least as of this writing is the Samsung Galaxy s20 series, which has to be the best phone during this time.

Samsung announced the Galaxy s20 series on February 11, 2020, which is the beast among its predecessors. Not much has changed in this series compare to the s10 series in terms of body design and some features.

Galaxy S20   Galaxy S20+   Galaxy S20 Ultra 5G

These devices came with upgraded hardware that led to its unique features, handy tips, and tricks, which this well-detailed user guide will govern you all through handling it. During reading further in this book, you will have insight into the s20 series specifications.

Chapter 2

What is inside the box

The galaxy s20 series is going to available in four different colors. Cloud Blue, Cosmic Gray, Cloud Pink, and Cosmic Black.

Let's open up the box and see what is inside.

You are going to get a knife and peel off the seal tape at the top edge. Lift the box, see what is inside. There is the phone, the super-fast 25-watt charger-

which allows your phone to charge super-fast. We also have the USB Type-C cable

that is going to connect to your charger thus, connect to the phone
to charge it and of course, we do have the type-C AKG wire

as you can see and is pretty good for tone. We also have a bunch
of air tips for the actual air bud (AKG wire).

Now, let's direct our attention to the Samsung galaxy s20 series
but ultra-precisely. Take off the plastic protector on the back and
get around about the body design.

Alright, the very first thing we are going to do is to take a close
look at the camera. We have a rectangular camera patch in the
back. I do want to mention the back, and the front display is made
out of gorilla glass six construction. It is nicely shinning, but it does

pick fingerprints easily. Inside below, we have th 100x hybrid zoom camera, right on top we have the 12-megapixel super wide-angle camera, and on top, we have a 108-megapixel primary camera and over here right next to the ultra-wide, we have 0.3-megapixel depth vision camera, and right on top, we have the flash.

Now around the bottom, we have the speaker row, the USB Type-C port, and the microphone. On the left side, we have absolutely nothing. On the top of the device, we have the sim card tray, another microphone, and on the right side, we have a volume rocker and the actual side keys. That is the actual tour around the device design. Very simple as expected.

Chapter 3

Specifications

Processor

The Samsung s20 series came with SNAPDRAGON 865 OR EYNOS 990. Depending on where you live.

Storage capacity

The phone also came with a baseline of 128GB ROM + 12GB RAM on s20, 128/512GB + 12GB RAM on s20 plus and 128GB ROM + 12GB RAM/512GB ROM + 16GB RAM across the board.

S20	128GB + 12GB
S20+	128/512GB + 12GB
S20 ULTRA	128GB + 12GB/ 512GB + 16GB

Battery capacity, charging and display

The phone featured different battery capacities depending on the module. From 4000mah for s20, 4500mah for s20 plus and 5000mah for the s20 ultra.

S20	4000 mAh
S20+	4500 mAh
S20 ULTRA	5000 mAh

The s20 and s20 plus featured 25Watts fast charger, and the s20 ultra has the 45Watts fast charger.

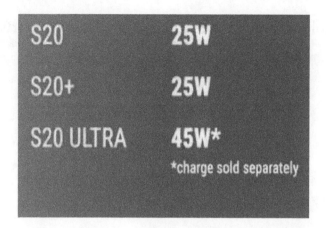

S20	25W
S20+	25W
S20 ULTRA	45W*
	*charge sold separately

Don't let us forget about the display. It is a big deal on s20, and three different screen sizes are depending on their module.

S20	6.2" / 120Hz
S20+	6.7" / 120Hz
S20 ULTRA	6.9" / 120Hz

All s20 modules came with a gorgeous 120Hz AMOLED display that bordered its smooth and refraction rate on camera and was ones only a feature only seen on high-end gaming phones.

Colour, headphone jack, charging and sim ports

GALAXY S20	GALAXY S20+	GALAXY S20 ULTRA
COSMIC GREY	COSMIC GREY	COSMIC GREY
CLOUD BLUE	**CLOUD BLUE**	COSMIC BLACK
CLOUD PINK	COSMIC BLACK	

Cloud pink is exclusive to the s20, cloud blue is available on the s20 and s20 plus, and the s20 ultra only comes in cosmic blue and cosmic black.

Say Goodbye headphone jack it is gone with the resurrection of s20 series.

The Type-C charging port serves as the headphone jack. Besides the charging port, there is a hole for the microphone, and the other side is the speaker.

At the top, there is another microphone and a sim/SD up to 1TB port.

Chapter 4

How to Install your sim & SD card

Now you have your Samsung galaxy s20 series. Let's look at how to get a sim & SD card install on it.

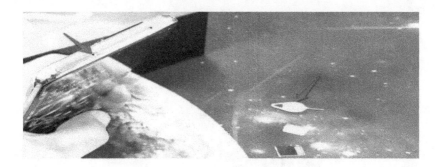

The first thing is this, quite look on top of your phone. We have the sim card/SD card tray; they are both in one tray. Patiently grab your sim ejector pin that came with your phone. If you don't have this, you can use another phone sim ejector. Check the tiny hole on the left and not the microphone,

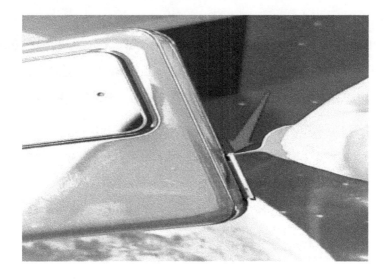

put the pin and give it a little bit pressure. Let the lip propel. There is a small tiny lip pull it out with your finger. Now if you look at the tray,

we have an area for an SD card and the other for a sim card. What you want to do is to make sure you see the hole for the pin is on the bottom left inside. Now go ahead and grab your SD card first. Don't forget that the maximum size for the s20 series is 1terabite. The previous s10 was 512GB, which is double can size the s20 series. Anyways, let's go ahead and put the SD just look at the tray and place the SD press with a little bit pressure to fit in perfectly. Now grab the sim card you can see on the left top hand side there is a bit diagonal slit around the corner you are going to make sure the sim card is going to stay right there. Place the sim card right on top and press down a little bit to snaps in place. Turn the tray over and make sure it doesn't come out.

Go ahead and grab your phone, slide in gently if it comes down a little bit, pull back and re-insert one of the cards. The hole on the tray and the one on the phone must tally.

NOTE: The SD card port can as well use as sim card port if and only if you want to use two sim cards and no SD.

Chapter 5

How to transfer data from your old device

While you are setting up your device, you will have this screen where you will be asking if you want to copy data from an old device or you want to start fresh.

Before you can copy data from your old device, the very first thing you will do is download a smart switch on your old device from google store.

To continue with your old device data on your new s20 series tap on copy data, wait for the device to update smart switch on your new device. On the next screen, you will be asking how do you want to connect your devices. Do not fret, just tap on wireless and agree to the pop-up.

Open smart switch on your old device to connect, tap on agree, and allow all the permissions. On the next screen, tap on send to send data to your new device, then tap on wireless, and the two phones will communicate with one another. On your new device, select what files you want to copy from the old device. You can select everything or otherwise be specific on files to copy, then scroll down on the new device and tap on transfer.

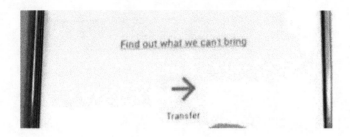

On your old device, tap on a copy then input your security to every command. On your new device, input the google account details on your old device, wait for verification, and all your data and account details will be transferred to your new device.

Chapter 6

How to set up the device

Now let's turn on the phone and set up for the very first time. Alright, you have turned on the phone for the very first time, now tap on the speaker logo at the top right corner to turn off the Bixby that talks as you set up the phone.

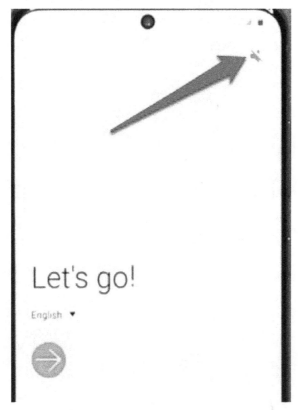

If you want voice guidance, make sure you enable the speaker logo.

Alright, tap on; let's go to see the next interface. The first thing you are to do here is to select all the bullets options except for the optional one.

Main Specs:

Snapdrgon 865 CPU

12GB of RAM

128GB of Storage

FOUR Rear Cameras

40MP Front Camera

IP68 Water Resistance

Wireless Powershare

Click on next, and you will be shown to add a network. Connect your WIFI to the phone if it requires a password, input your password, and click connect and if not, click connect to continue with the setup. Alright, the next thing is checking for updates; it might take a couple of seconds here. Meanwhile, I do want to let you know we do have a 40-megapixel at the top in the middle. Only ultra-featured this while the s20 and s20+ feature 10-megapixel camera.

Now, the next thing is to copy apps and data from an existing device by tapping next or don't copy if you want to set up a brand-new device. The next thing is to add your Google account, input your email and password then click next. Wait for some seconds to fetch your account information from the server. Tap on next

Now let's see about google assistant. You are all good to go. If your google account has already been set up, then click on more then accept for everything on google in row quick. And if you are yet to set it up, do read the information display and select your choices.

Change your device name

The name of your device is what attach to your Bluetooth name, Wi-Fi name, whenever they are turned on. It made it easy to recognize the name of your phone and also a nice touch of personalization.

- Go to settings
- Scroll down
- Tap on about phone
- Tap on edit and input your desired name

Chapter 7

Lock screen setup

Samsung s20 series is the most secured device the company has ever made is the first to feature a new secured processor called THE GORDON SHAPE to protect against horrible tasks similar to the google is being put in the pixel phones.

In other to set up your lock screen, swipe down on the screen and tap on Settings, scroll down and tap on the lock screen to select the lock screen type. Under this, you will see the following options

- **Swipe:** When you select this as your lock screen type, you only need just a swipe on your phone screen to unlock it. It is not advisable to use this type of lock screen due to no form of security in it.
- **Pattern:** This type of lock screen is widespread on Android devices.

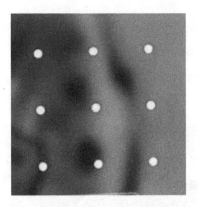

It is a form of lock screen in which you have to secure your phone by making a line drawn on targeted areas.

- **Pin:** A pin is a form of security lock that has to do with digits. Back then,

it comprises of only four-digit numbers, and with vast in technology, you can add up to twelve-digit numbers. To input your pin, swipe up on the lock screen.

- **None:** If you select this action, you will access your home screen immediately when you press the side key.

Chapter 8

Device security

Face unlock recognition

Even though the Galaxy s20 modules don't feature dedicated sensors on the front for facial scanning, they still have the options for face recognition. Face unlock is more even convenient and is just a feature you should only be aware of because technically, this doesn't have any 3D depth sensor which isn't as secure as face ID.

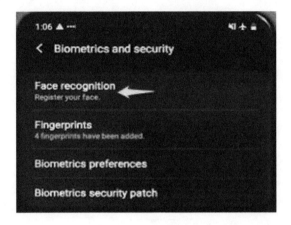

To enable this feature, what you are going to do is go into your settings, check biometric and security, then tap on it, tap on face recognition, input your pin then tap continue.

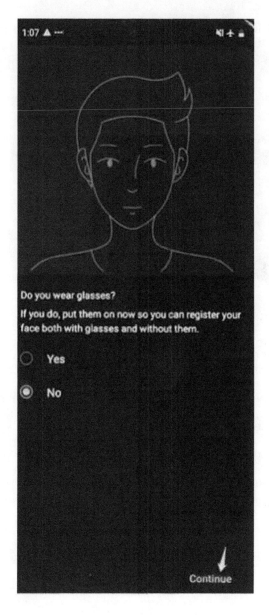

If you do wear glasses tick YES, then put on the glasses to register your faces with glasses or without them, and if you don't do wear

glasses, tick NO to record only your bare face. Tap on continue, wait some seconds to register your face, then click done.

From there, you can add an alternative lock that will help if you have someone else that might need to get into your phone like your significant other or maybe a relative. You can scan their face, and then they can get into your phone using face recognition. Ones all these are enabled, make sure face unlock is on, or it should automatically turn on itself. If it happens, you wear glasses one day or sometimes a wig you can scan your identity using those things as well so that it will recognize you.

Fix fingerprint issue

If you are having a tough time with your fingerprint scanner, follow these few recommendations that might work for you, and improve your usability.

After every big system update, make sure you delete your current fingerprint and re-adjustable them.

Increase touch sensitivity if you are using a third-party screen protector (settings, display, touch sensitivity)

Register the phone fingerprint multiple time and try to avoid repeating the same path each time you register.

Google play protect

Google implemented google play protect while back to help avoid more malware and other harmful applications from been install on the device. Generally speaking, Google protects works in the background as you download apps, but you can majorly scan your system if you want to.

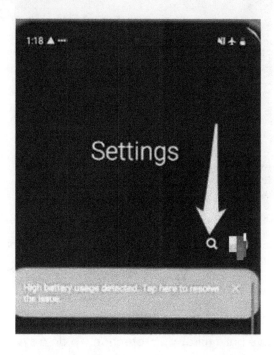

To enjoy this feature, all you need is go to settings, tap on biometric and security and then tap on google play protect. You can also use the search bar in the settings to navigate this feature.

Just type google play protect, tap on it and then tap on google play protect again, and later on the next interface, you tap on the settings logo at the top right corner.

Over there, we have two different settings Scan apps with play protect, Improve harmful apps protection. To do a system scan and check the condition of your apps, refresh with the logo beside "looks good."

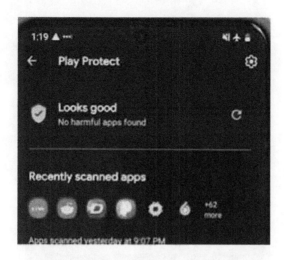

Samsung pass

If you are looking for a free pass manager that fast in secure, Samsung pass is excellent. It manages your passport, payment information all secured by fingerprint and face authentication, but unfortunately, there is no desktop in the face, but I can figure how to access it.

Bounce into the settings, and tap on the search icon, search for Samsung pass. Over there, there are three options one for fingerprint one for face recognition and the last for biometric and security.

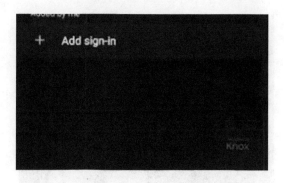

Tap on the one under biometric and security then tap on Samsung pass again. Setup your Samsung pass and add sign in details of websites or applications you wish to use Samsung pass to access. Tap on the three dots to go into the settings to activate the biometric to authenticate Samsung pass identity.

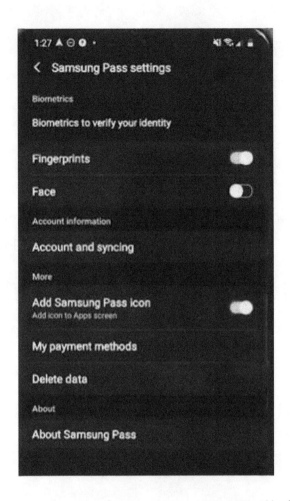

The fingerprint is registered as soon as you register. Under this, you can add the Samsung app icon to your desktop and app screen. You can also add a payment method to your Samsung, and of course, you can delete all of your Samsung pass data.

Samsung blockchain Keystore

Samsung has been using the combination of hardware and software android devices for security purposes known as KNOX. It is no more news; they've been using it for years; however, add somewhat new features within the settings called Samsung BLOCKCHAIN KEYSTORE. It's meant to be for professional business investors and other people that might be venturing into cryptocurrency.

Another way to go into the device search without having to go into the settings is to pull up your app drawer, tap on search, and input blockchain. It is just like it does when you search from settings.

Welcome to Samsung Blockchain Keystore

A secure and convenient place for your cryptocurrency

Learn more

To continue, read and agree to the Terms and Conditions.

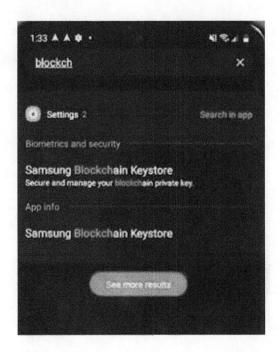

It might save you a little bit of time, but I just want to teach you both ways. Tap on Samsung blockchain Keystore, tap on it again, then agree and continue the setup.

You can either import an existing digital wallet which supports cryptocurrency, or you create a new one.

Secure your folder

If you are having any documents, files, apps, or anything else on your phone you want to keep private, then you should probably check out the secure folder. It allows you to store things and set up a folder, and in other to gain access to the content, you need to verify your identity through either biometrics or maybe an account password. Best of all, if you log in to your Samsung cloud account on your laptop or desktop computer, you gain access to everything that's stored within that folder.

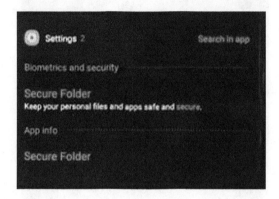

In other to turn on the secure folder, go ahead to the search bar and then type in a secure folder, tap secure folder under settings then tap secure folder again, pick a verification method to use, tap on next, input your selected identity, tap continue and do it one more time for verification

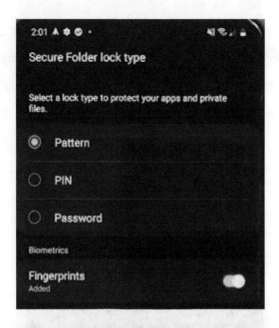

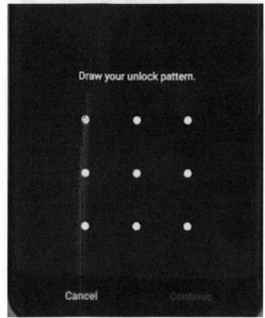

73

By default, it will store your gallery, calendar events, contacts, camera, internet (browsed history, passwords, etc.), my files, and Samsung notes. You can also add various apps, including third-party apps, to your secure folder.

You can also add different files including images, videos, audio, documents and my files (browse your file structure and find different things like your download folder, etc.)

Secure Wi-Fi

Here is another cool security feature. Samsung equips all of its phones with the settings known SECURE WI-FI, which is a glorify VPN, but you get it for free.

Go ahead and search for secure Wi-Fi from your search bar, tap on the option under settings, tap on secure Wi-Fi one more time, and is going to take you to your account page.

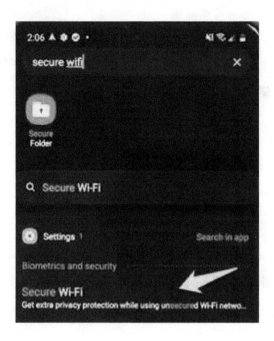

Here, you can either upgrade your account to get more data. Tap on protect to run the VPN. You can check your protection plan; this is where you upgrade your account. You can also check on your protected apps, which can be enabled or disable and also check on your protection history.

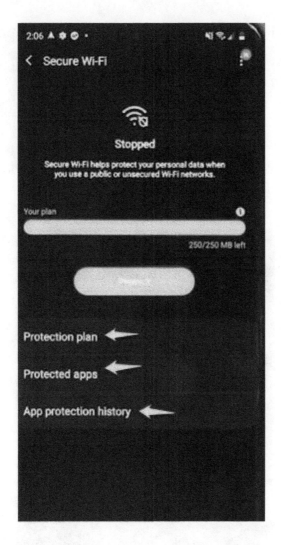

There are other settings you need to be aware of. Tap on the three dots in the top right corner.

Auto protect Wi-Fi: You can have it automatically turn ON whenever you connect to any Wi-Fi networks

Trusted Wi-Fi networks: you can customize its experience by trusting some Wi-Fi networks while not trusting others.

Use location information: This enables us to use or block location information.

Show icon on the home screen: Enable this to have access to secure Wi-Fi on the home screen quickly.

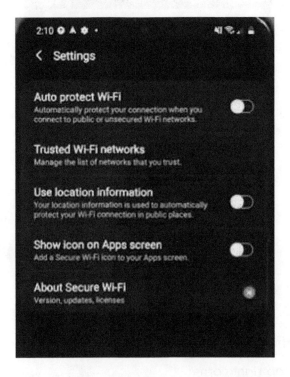

Encrypt and Decrypt Sound Disk Card

Samsung makes it possible to encrypt and decrypt your SD card, which you have or have not to store any vital information on it.

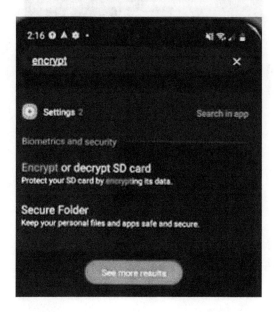

Head into the search bar and search for encrypt, tap on it, a brief explanation on the feature is shown. Take a moment to read the information then tap on encrypt SD.

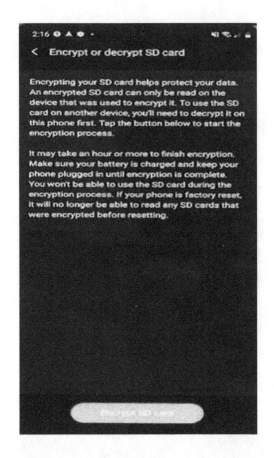

If another way round, you want to decrypt your SD card, follow the same procedures, and tap on decrypt SD.

Pin windows (child mode)

If you are a parent and you do attend to occasional, which facilitates giving your phone to kids to play with or watch movies while you take care of some grown full business, you are going to love to pin windows. It is super useful and is going to protect your kid from wandering places on your phone that he/she shouldn't as avoid getting anything useful accidentally deleted.

Pin windows (child mode)

Go ahead and do a search for pin window from your search bar, tap on pin window then toggle it to ON pin window.

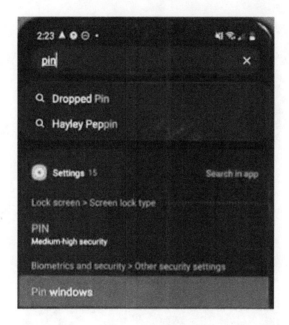

To check pin window application, go to the recent apps, tap on the app icon you wish to allow pin window, tap on pin this app, a pop-up will come up, tap ok, and the app is pinned.

The only way to get out of the app is to swipe up and hold the pinned app, and the phone will lock then unlock to leave the app.

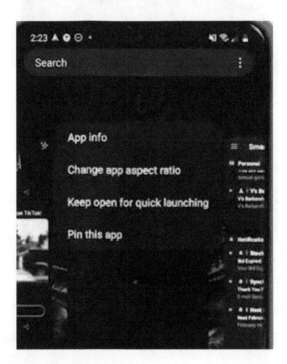

Customize your app permission

Sometimes the app you are using might gain access to something on your phone that is questionable. For example, maybe you download the podcaster app without knowing better, you give information to use the cameras. Many didn't know this information can be changed after you have downloaded the app and then agreed to everything.

Go to the search bar and do a search for permissions, and right there, you have a location for app permissions, app permission manager, and then privacy permission manager.

Tap on app permission manager, and you have all of the different permissions that you have on your phone such as;

- ➢ Body sensor
- ➢ call log
- ➢ camera
- ➢ contacts
- ➢ location
- ➢ microphone
- ➢ phone
- ➢ physical activity
- ➢ SMS
- ➢ Storage
- ➢ Additional permission
  - ○ Car information
  - ○ Read instant messages
  - ○ Write instant messages

You can just go through say you tap on the camera and check what apps you allowed to use your camera.

Disable any app that you found a little bit suspicious, and you don't want them to have access to your camera.

Go back to permission under the location you can do the same thing. Check what apps are using your location services, and again, if you feel that app should not have access to that information, just turn it off.

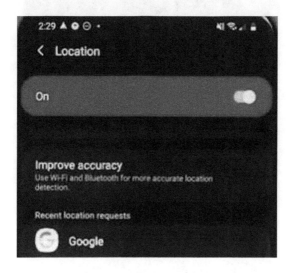

Personalize your contents

Here is a huge deal, but if you are sketchy about Google, Samsung, and everyone in between knowing your location, your likes, and dislikes, etc. disabling customization services might help you sleep a little bit better at night.

Customization services allowed Goggle and Samsung to use your personal information, whether through your used pardons, location, call history and to the voice services and deliver customs ads app in another suggestion base after that information.

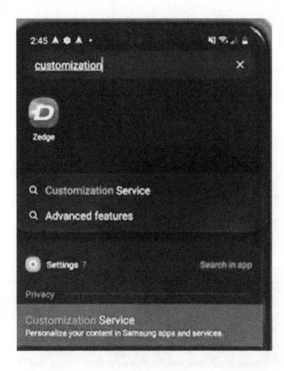

Go ahead to search bar and do a search for customization, then tap on customization service, tap on customization service one more.

By default, it may, and it may not be automatically turn on just depends on what you enabled while during the setup process. If It is already turned on, disable customization service, customization ads, and marketing and then turn off all devices. Tap on turn off o the pop-up.

Now the customization service is completely turn off.

Clear your customization service log

If you choose to disable the services and they are ON by default. What you are going to do is go back to the customization service, tap on erase personal data, tap on erase, and verify your identity.

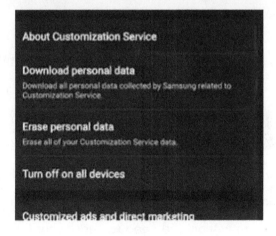

Trusted devices to unlock

If you tend to use several Bluetooth devices throughout the day like the watch, headphones, etc. you may be looking into trusted devices that might save you a little bit of time when it comes to getting inside your phone. You can make any device that is connected to your phone trusted devices, which simply means when your phone is connected to that specific device, you can unlock your phone without the need to verify your ID.

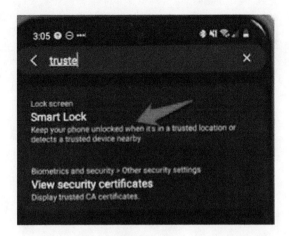

Typically, by default, when you connect a Bluetooth device, you get a notification asking you if you want to trust the device. Just in case it doesn't happen to you, go into the settings and do a search for trusted devices, tap on it and tap on the smart lock again, enter your pin, tap on trusted devices, tap on add trusted device, and you pick the device you want to trust then tap add on the pop-up.

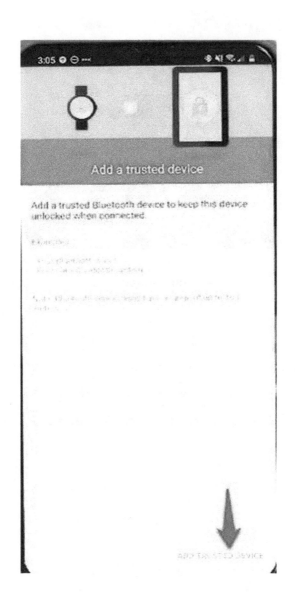

Trusted places

Another way of getting in your pone a little bit faster is by using trusted places. What you do is to assign a specific location within the settings. Whenever your phone gets into the vicinity of that location, you no longer require to input your passcode or your fingerprint.

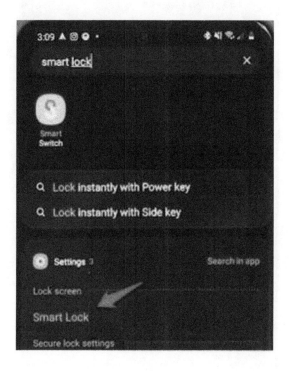

Just like trusted devices, a trusted location is also under smart lock. Go to search bar, and search for smart lock, tap on smart lock under the lock screen settings, tap on the smart lock again, input your pin if activated, tap on trusted places, tap on your present location then update to add as trusted place. It will automatically pick the location of your current place.

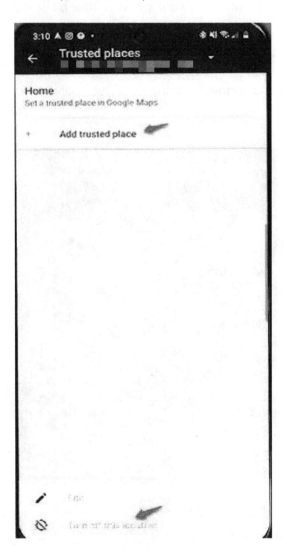

On-body protection

The last way of getting into your phone just a little bit quicker is enabling on-body detection.

These allow your phone sensor to detect if your phone is in your purse, pocket, backpack, bag. If it detects these things, then you are not required to enter any passcode or verification to get inside your phone. Speeding up the process a little bit.

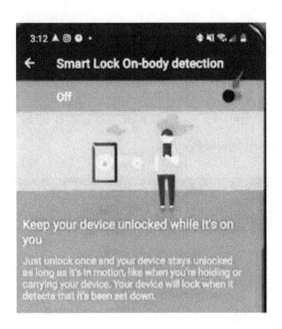

Just like trusted devices and trusted places, on-body detection is also under the smart lock section just go through the previous procedures, tap on-body detection, toggle ON, tap Continue on the pop-up.

Chapter 9

Find my device

Some may not know this is a way to track your device within the settings. Enabling it allows you to track your device and perform other options should in case you lost your phone or stolen.

To activate this feature, go into settings, tap on biometric and security, locate find my mobile and tap on it, and you have the option to find my mobile and turn it ON.

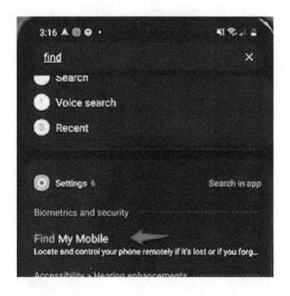

You can also access this feature if you go into your search bar and do a search for find my mobile, tap on find my mobile, and you are good to go.

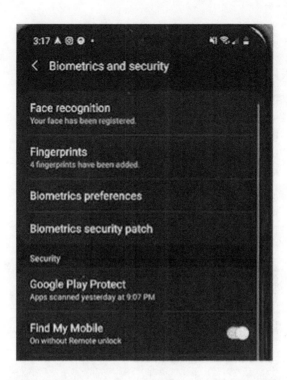

When you tap on find my mobile, you have a couple of other settings such as

Remote unlock: This a great feature, in case you forget your pin or password you will able to unlock your phone remotely and access the same Samsung without losing any of your data. Do enable it.

Send the last location: This is a good one in case you lost your device or stolen. Do enable it.

Add contact information on the lock screen

In case you lost your phone, and someone finds it and doesn't know who to contact because the device will be lockdown and the founder will not able to get inside of it.

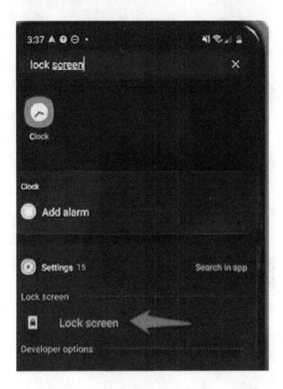

Go into your search bar and do a search for lock screen, then tap on it, scroll down to contact information and do a tap on it and then write the information you want it to display on the lock screen.

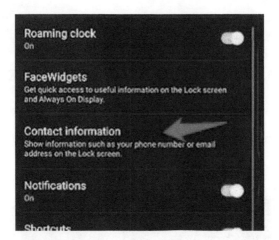

May be for example "if lost contact xxx-xxx-xxxx". Add a contact that is saved for them to call in other to get in contact with you.

Secure lock settings

This is an essential feature for protecting your phone data against someone who stole your phone. This feature can have your phone automatically perform a reset after 15 incorrect login attempts.

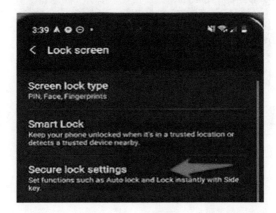

To set it up, go back into the lock screen settings, and ten locate secure lock settings and tap on it, input your ID if activated, and here you have the option for auto factory reset, tap on it to enable it.

Chapter 10

Enhance home screen display

Bring back the power button

By default, if you long-press the side-key, it launches the Bixby application. So, it is not possible to deliver the power off option display.

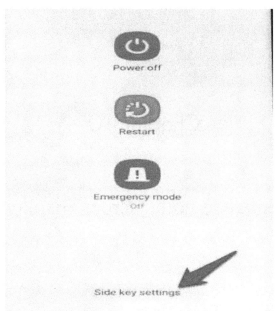

To turn off the phone, slide down the notification panel and tap on the power icon or go to the side key settings from the screen, then change the phone option for the side key to show the power off option when you long-press it.

Enable/disable gesture navigation

Again, by default, Samsung likes to employ its classic navigation buttons on the bottom of the screen, but if you go to the settings, display follows by navigation bar, you can enable full-screen gestures.

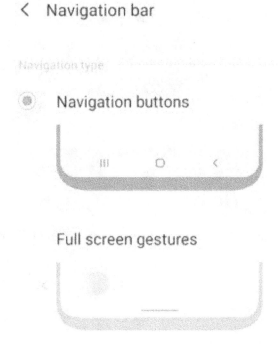

You can just swipe on the screen side to go back and swipe up on the screen to go home or swipe and hold to see the multitasking view on the screen. You can also disable this feature to use full-screen mode.

Getting more apps to your home screen

If you long-press the wallpaper on your home screen

you have the home screen settings at the bottom tap on it, and you see an option to change the home screen layout and number of rows and columns for applications.

Home screen grid
5X6

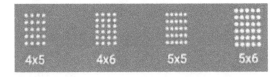

Choose the home screen grid option and select the layout that you want.

Chapter 11

Wi-Fi calling

Wi-Fi calling enables you to receive or make calls over a wireless internet connection. It doesn't undergo a traditional telecommunication provider. If you are in an area where the usual calling network is weak or unavailable, Wi-Fi calling is an alternative to make voice calls.

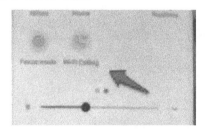

To activate or enable Wi-Fi calling on your s20 series is quite simple and amazing. The method to activate this feature is the same thing for all modules ranging from the s20 to the s20 ultra.

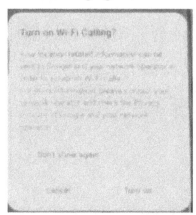

All you need is your s20 with a sim card installed from a service provider that supports it, something like AT&T, T-Mobile, Verizon. Connect your phone over a Wi-Fi, and you don't need to go much into the settings swipe down to notification tiles panel, swipe left to locate the Wi-Fi calling logo, toggle it on, and response to the pop-up with turn on.

Depending on whether it is time to use it, you will see the calling symbol next to the Wi-Fi icon, but don't worry, you may not see it there, but Wi-Fi calling is activated.

Here is another method to activate Wi-Fi calling.

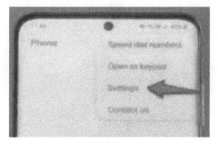

Go to the phone app, tap the three vertical dots at the right top corner, tap on Settings, scroll down, and here you have Wi-Fi calling to enable.

How to enable battery percentage

If by default, the battery percentage isn't shown in the status bar, you can save the stress of swiping down the notification panel to check battery meter.

- Swipe down the notification panel twice
- Tap on the three dots

- Select status bar

- Toggle on the show battery percentage

Activate landscape mode

This feature will allow you to work in landscape on your Samsung s20 series. To activate this feature, long-press your home screen wallpaper as you did earlier,

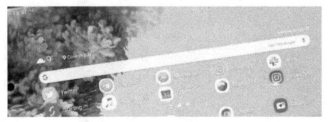

Rotate to landscape mode
Rotate the Home screen automatically when your phone's orientation changes

scroll down and look for rotate to landscape mode. Toggle on this option to enable it. Now when you turn your phone horizontally, the layout of your phone shows landscape display , and when you toggle off, it disables the feature.

Switch off Samsung daily

To the left of your home screen is a field called **Samsung daily**. It is full of all kinds of areas from news media and other services.

To switch it off, long press on the home screen wallpaper and then swipe to the right then toggle off to switch off Samsung daily.

Toggle on to activate Samsung daily.

Swipe down notification anywhere

These allow you to access your notifications and tiles bar quickly and efficiently, considering the display size of the phone.

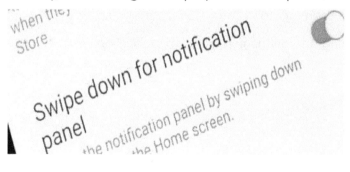

Go back to your home screen settings by long-pressing the home screen wallpaper and tap the home screen settings option. Scroll down and tap on swipe down for notification settings. Now, the notification panel shows whenever you swipe down anywhere on the home screen.

All apps on the home screen

So, if you draw all your applications on the home screen, all apps will be seen on different docks after the first dock is fully depending on how numerous your applications are.

You can access these settings on the home screen just choose home screen layout and then select Home screen only
and all your apps will be spread across over the home screen rather than in the app drawer.

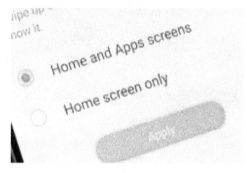

If you are using the app draw, you can alphabetize your apps.

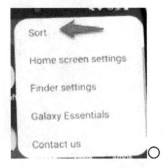

Open the app drawer and tap on the little dots on the top corner
to open the menu.

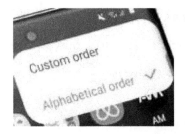

Tap sort, and you can choose alphabetical order, and all your apps
will automatically sort themselves out alphabetically.

Tap to show a fingerprint scanner

You can have your fingerprint icon to illuminate while your phone is sleep and lock by tapping your phone to know where it is to unlock it.

Head into settings, scroll down, and tap on biometrics and security then fingerprint. Type in your pin or password and head to show the icon when the screen is off. Tap on this, and you have these three options

- **On always ON display**
- **Tap to show**
- **None**

Select tap to show to activate this feature.

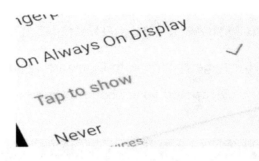

ige̶r

On Always On Display ✓

Tap to show

Never

Refresh rate and Quad HD resolution

By default, the Samsung display is set to 60Hz. But if you want a high refresh rate for all to smooth and animation rate go to settings, display, motion smoothness then chooses 120Hz.

60 Hz   120 Hz

Adjust your screen's refresh rate.

High refresh rate (120 Hz)
Get more realistic animations and smoother scrolling.

Standard refresh rate (60 Hz)
Get a longer battery life.

You can only choose this if the screen resolution is set to FHD.

To access the screen resolution settings, head to settings, display then screen resolution, and select WQHD+. Samsung default resolution is FHD+, which hinders having smoothness and refresh rate of 120Hz.

Enabling Quad HD resolution is ok if you are on s20, but on the plus and ultra, you might not want to show up the experience.

Select a resolution. Some currently running apps may close when you change the resolution.

HD+   **FHD+**   WQHD+

1600 x 720   **2400 x 1080**   3200 x 1440

As soon as you choose the WQHD+, it will switch the refresh rate to 60Hz.

High refresh rate isn't supported in WQHD+. Your screen will change to standard refresh rate.

OK

It is quite complicated to select out of smoothness and screen resolution.

Chapter 12

Camera and its properties

Rebuilding the Samsung Galaxy s20 series camera from the ground up, even the s10 series camera was pretty great already. The new s20 series smartphone is just pretty great and amazing. There is a lot to talk about like larger image sensors that let in more light, the ability to zoom in the photo than before, 8K and 4K video capture, single take mode, and 33-megapixel screen capture from video.

The s20 ultra featured five cameras, including the 40-megapixel on the front. The hybrid zoom camera, 12-megapixel super wide-angle camera, 108-megapixel primary camera, 3D-depth sensor camera, and a flash.

The s20 and s20 plus came with four cameras, including the 10-megapixels on the front.

The 64-megapixels telephoto, 12-megapixels wide and ultra-wide angle.

Bigger image sensors

Since the release of the S6 sensor size, Galaxy S series primary camera has stayed the same size. In 2020, it gets a significant upgrade, and that's a good thing as a bigger image sensor determines a better image camera.

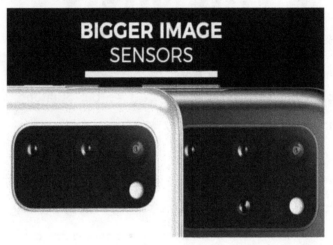

The improvements are cross table also enough to the camera wide-angle, telephoto, and ultra-wide angle. The s20 ultra with it 108-megapixel camera has an even larger sensor. Currently the largest in the market as of the writing of this book. Some might be thinking plenty of megapixels is excellent if you make a lot of large print, but I have a practice for the everyday user.

By default, photos taking at for 108-megapixels images instead every 9-pixels are fused into one, so you end up with one photo with plenty of details.

Samsung called this process **NONA BINNING.**

NONA BINNING

Many approaches are on similar devices, but Samsung is pretty bullish about the tech that is on s20.

Before we move on, lets briefly discuss the selfie camera. Apart from been moved from the top right to the top center, the s20, s20+, and s20 ultra have only one selfie camera.

On paper, it looks like the same selfie camera as last year. For even more resolution, the s20 ultra has a 40-megapixel front camera.

100X Zoom

Another focus area for Samsung was the zoom. On the s20 and s20 plus, you get 3x optical zoom and up to 30x hybrid zoom, and on the s20 ultra, there is something called **SPACE ZOOM** giving you 10x last optical zoom and up to a 100x hybrid zoom.

How to hide the front camera

Samsung made the front camera cut-out tiny, but if the body is hidden behind the fake bezel, you can do that.

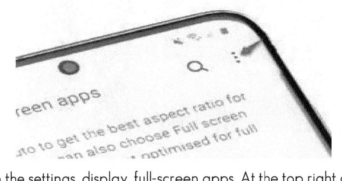

Open the settings, display, full-screen apps. At the top right corner, tap on the three dots, which is the menu to reveal the advance settings.

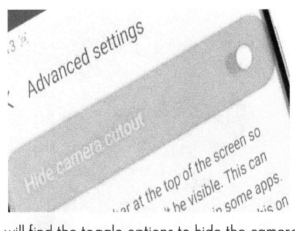

Here, you will find the toggle options to hide the camera. Switch it on, and it looks like it does not even there.

Connect 8KQLED TV and 8k video capture

Finally, video capture also gets the same major upgrade. 8k video capture at 24 frames per secs is now possible.

Perfect view also has Samsung QLED 8K TV because now you have the device that shoots 8K contents that you can view on it and be able to cast.

It is also now easier all you have to do is to tap your phone on the TV.

Pick moments from video in 33-megapixels

Now, because you are shooting a video in such a high resolution, the galaxy s20 lets you pick your favorite moment on the same video and store as a 33-megapixels photo.

From the gallery app, just crop through the video and pick the frame that you like. You can also create a Gif file from the video.

How to move the shutter button on the screen

We have discussed the specifications of the camera in the last chapter. Now let check on how to handle its features.

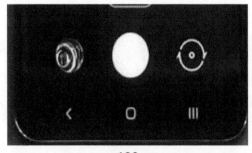

When you launch the camera, you have the shutter button at the bottom center of the screen, which may not be very convenient all the time, especially based on how you handle your phone.

What you can do is that it is moveable to any part of the screen. All that you need is press hold and drag to anywhere on the screen for easy use.

When you are done with the camera, you can drag it back to its initial position.

Optical and hybrid zoom application

On the bottom of the camera box, these are the shortcut to jump around between the three lenses. The double middle tree
, the icon is wide-angle, and the left three icons are the ultra-wide-angle while the single three on the right is the telephoto.

At the bottom, you notice the addition zoom choice, which can be zoom up to 30x On s20 and s20 plus, but s20 ultra can be zoom up to 100x.

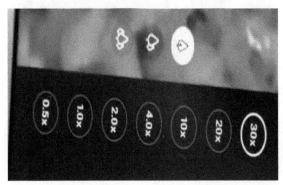

With so many zoom options, how does one get to the desire zoom point.? It is pretty easy, click any of the trees as mentioned, and on the side, you get options to pick the level of zoom.

Single take mode

Another nifty software features called **SINGLE TAKE MODE.** When a moment is taking place, and you can't quite figure it out if you want to take a photo or shoot a video, but with this feature, you can do both at a goal.

All you have to do is to switch to the single take mode, and the phone will capture photos and video simultaneously for 10 seconds.

Once you are done, it will then offer you a curation of the best moment.

How to record 8k and 4k video

With the s20 series, you can shoot video at 8k and 4k quality. These allow the video to have a UHD display.

To record 8k or 4k video, dive into the camera settings by tapping the settings logo at the top left corner, scroll down to rear video size, and tap on it, and you have different sizes to capture videos.

The first one is the 8k option, which video record is limited to 5 minutes.

The 4k option is seen under resolution.

These same features are available for the front camera.

Chapter 13

Edge screen setup

These are animation colors that display around the edge of the screen whenever there is notification and also a quick bar to access different applications.

Edge lightning

- Go to settings
- Tap on display and scroll down to edge lightning
- Scroll down to edge screen and toggle on
- Tap on edge lightning
- Tap lightning style to enable it (This will show the effect when u receive any notification). You can also take different types of effects.
- Tap on done to activate effects

Edge panel

- Go to settings
- Tap on display and scroll down to edge lightning
- Scroll down to edge screen and toggle on
- Tap on edge panel
- Tap on the three dots
- Tap on handle settings to change lock handle position and colors.

Chapter 14

Advanced features of the s20 series

Now let's dive into the advanced features of Samsung galaxy s20 series. The very first thing you are to do is swipe down to the notification panel, click on the settings/logo at the top right corner. Or you look for the settings application, allow the phone to show the settings interface, scroll down, and you will see the advance features tap on it.

Under this, there are lots of features we will be looking into in this chapter. Mind you, some features such as; **Bixby Routine, Call & text on other devices, Link to Windows** will be discussed in detail in another chapter.

Double press

To activate these features, enable the double press option.

After you might have tapped on advanced features, tap on the side key, which is the first on the list at the top. Of course, side key means the single key before the volume rocker also

Known as the power button.

On the norm, if you press the key just one-time, it locks the screen. If you double press the button, it will launch an application, or you can choose to start the quick launch camera. So basically, you can just double-tap the button and boom! The camera launches, and that's great for a quick shot. Some people like Bixby, so if you select open Bixby and you double press the button, it will launch Bixby application. We are going to discuss in detail **"what is Bixby?"** in its chapter.

There is another option under the double press, which is unique. If you use an application often, you can quickly access the application if you select an open app option, and you double press the side key.

To select and save an app to use, tap the settings ⚙ logo beside open app, and select.

Press and hold

Alright, if you press and hold the side key, you can wake up Bixby, or you can alternate the power off menu. So, if you press and hold the side key, it will show the power off menu interface. If you select wake Bixby and if you press and hold the side key, it will open the Bixby application.

"If you select wake Bixby, how will you gonna power off your phone.?"

NOTE: When you swipe down to the notification panel, there is a power logo ⏻ beside the settings logo ⚙ . Press it to show the power off the interface. Furthermore, you can only disable double press if you don't want to use it.

Screenshot and screen recorder

This is a fantastic feature where you can either take a screenshot or record the screen.

Under this section, we have;

Screenshot toolbar

So, every time you take a screenshot by pressing the power button and the volume down it will give a screenshot and a screenshot toolbar below

Where all these features on the toolbar allow you to edit the screenshot on the go. Screenshot the full information on a page at a time, tap on this icon [icon] and it will be saved in your gallery. If you like to add a hashtag to your screenshot, you can get this done by tapping this logo [#]. If you want to crop or draw on your screenshot, kindly tap this logo [icon]. Another feature of this screenshot toolbar is that you can share your screenshot instantly and delete automatically after it has been shared. To do this, tap on this logo [<].

You can also select the format you want your screenshot to be saved. We have the JPG, which is the most accessible format and most shareable format in the world and the PNG.

Screen recorder settings

With this, you can record the screen of the device when you tap on it. You will have all the settings under it.

If you select no sound you will record the screen with no sound, but if you choose media sound, the screen will record media audio in the phone, or if you select the last option which is media sound and mic, it will pick your voice or any external voice outside around the phone.

There are also options for you to select the video quality of your choice. We have the **1080p, 720p and 480p.**

To record the screen, swipe down to the notification panel and here you will see the screen recorder feature

Screen recorder Enable it, then you click allow for anything they ask for, and then you choose from the sound options, the press starts recording. It will countdown three then after, and the screen record will start. You will notice a toolbar on the screen which is not visible in the record. To stop the screen record, do tap on this logo and the file is saved to your gallery. Go to your gallery and check screen recording to view your saved work.

Motion and gestures

Lift to wake up

This feature allows your device to wake up whenever it is lifted. If you enable this feature, your device will wake up automatically when lifting.

Double-tap to wake

This feature has been in android devices for some years. If you have this enabled, whenever you double-tap on the screen, it will come up

Smart stay

Smart key keeps the screen on while you're looking at it. If you enable this feature, your screen will be on while starring at it until you are done looking at it.

Smart alert

The smart alert is another fantastic feature that gives feedback on the notification(s). If your phone screen is turned over down and you have missed notification(s), it will vibrate when lifting a little bit but if it doesn't vibrate it shows no missed notification.

Easy mute

If somebody calls you or alarm goes off, you can mute by placing your Hand over the screen or turn the screen face down.

Swipe Palm over screen to capture

With this feature, you can take a screenshot by swiping over the screen. It will save the stress of using the buttons feature. Mind you; this feature will also work while the keyboard is available.

Swipe to call/send messages

Swipe to call/send messages allows you to make calls when you swipe right on contact and enables to send a message when you swipe left. This feature is fantastic.

One-handed mode

Another impressive feature is the one-handed mode. It allows you to scale under the display size to use the phone with one Hand. This feature is of two types; we have the button version, which is applicable when you double-tap the home button. It will make the screen smaller, which is easier to manage with one Hand. If you have a small hand, you can resize it to your satisfaction when you press and drag from the edge of the resized screen. To disable one-handed mode, tap on the black field. To use the gesture version, press and swipe down on the home button. To move it side to side tap on this logo .

Dual messengers or applications

This feature offers you to have two messenger applications because every app deserves its data. You can have two separate accounts on Facebook, WhatsApp and lot other messenger apps. Supported apps will be shown, and you enable it. It helps to operate two accounts at a go.

File transfer made easy

File transfer is another fantastic feature of Samsung galaxy s20 series, tap on it to enable it.

What happen is let assume you want to share something with anybody from your gallery, locate the picture or video, press and hold, tap on share ⏩ and if anybody is available for quick share is going to show right over here.

Make sure there is a nearby other Samsung device, and quick share is also enabled on it. This feature will allow you to share large files instantaneously while over your WI-FI connection.

Send SOS messages

Emergency message Is a vital feature if you want to make sure you are getting to take care of in case of an emergency. It could be anything, or somebody wants to bump on you. It can be used to send a quick message to a contact that you know will take action. So, what you do is to enable this and agree on the terms. Once you have allowed it, you have to add at least one recipient to send SOS message. Click on add and create a contact then save it.

Now if you press the side-key three times quickly the phone will take photos of your current situation with the front and back camera and also record an audio voice of your surroundings for 5-10 secs and send it through your emergency contact.

NOTE: *You can add multiple contacts*

Access your phone on your computer

This feature is effortless to activate. All you need is a window system (computer). If you enable this, you will be prompt to go to your windows PC download an application, and you will be able to project the entire form on to your window display. It's a very

148

sensitive feature but very easy to use. Connect your phone to your computer so that you can access your texts, notifications, recent photos and more

When you enable this, it will ask you to log in to your Microsoft account

NOTE: *This doesn't work with mac as of this writing*

Floating notifications

Floating notification is also an advanced feature that allows you to reply to notification(s) in a pop-up window. Whenever you received a notification, let assume an SMS the smart pop-up will be displayed on your screen. When you tap it going to expand, and you can respond as you please. You can also move it around like a window when you hold on its drag. You can also resize it to your satisfaction. It can also be minimized by tapping this logo and maximize with this logo . It can be enabled for various apps base on your needs.

NOTE: This is only available for apps that support multi-window.

Access your Calls and texts on other devices

Here is another similar feature but only works with other Samsung devices. You can call and text on other devices that also support this feature. As long you are logged in with same Samsung account when your phone rings the tablet will ring as well and able to take a call and respond to a text on that other device and they will be linked together using your Samsung account.

Chapter 15

Bixby

Automate tasks with Bixby routine

Bixby routines are "IF" and "ELSE" statement so basically, if you need a condition on your phone meets a condition your phone performs several functions that you defined. For example, we have some presets, let's tap on Good morning preset. You will see "if" the time is equal to 9 am (you set your prefered time) what you are to do is you tap on next "then" you want your phone to perform this functions, and again, all these functions can be removed, or you can add functions as you pleased.

Remember, because Bixby routine is automated, they only run when the condition is met. You don't have to do anything they run automatically in the background.

If you tap on this logo ⋮ at the top right corner, you see how to use. When you swipe down to the notification panel, it going to tell you this routine is running right now.

You can also go to settings to configure the followings;

- **Samsung Account**
- **Show Bixby Routine icon**
- **Customization Service and**
- **About Bixby Routine**

Activate Bixby quick command

Bixby quick comment is a single action or set of activities that can be activated with a word or a phrase. To access Bixby quick command, you going to go inside the Bixby app and make sure it is enabled but if you disabled Bixby, then you are not going to see inside the app. Another way to access Bixby is by using the start launcher. Swipe to the left on the home screen, there is Bixby voice pen as a card, tap on more, and it will take you to the same page then tap on the three dots right here and tap on quick command, and you will have two options name; Recommended & My commands.

Recommended are other recommended quick commands based on different categories such as;

- productivity
- daily routine
- lifestyle and place.

My commands are the set of commands you currently have run such as; the good morning command.

The quick command may not be for everybody, and this is just the stock recommended good morning quick command, and if you want to customize it to suit your satisfaction, there are couples of ways it can be done.

The first one is to tap on the good morning, which is the stock command. From there, you can remove and add commands.

Another method is by tapping on the three dots ⬛ and tap delete to remove the stock commands, tap on recommended go on daily routine tap on good morning then tap on edit. Now you can start taking away or add different actions that will take place whenever you say good morning. Tap on done to save your command.

So, that's a quick look at Bixby quick commands. There are also extremely useful for smart home control, especially if you are using Samsung appliances or you are tie in smart things equal.

Extract text with Bixby vision

You can access Bixby vision in two different ways.

The first one is to open the camera and tap on the settings logo at the left upper corner and is going to launch Bixby vision.

The second one is using voice to open Bixby vision through this command. Hey, Bixby, "open Bixby vision." Hold the side key and say the command.

You can do several different things with Bixby vision, including identifying objects, types of foods, plants and things like that but I will guide you on three different things I found a little bit more practical.

One of its features is the ability to extract the text of an object. For example, you want to scan your business card all you need is place the business card under your so it can be seen by the camera. Let Bixby vision scan it, and at the bottom, you have an option to extract the text, tap on it and wait for some mins/secs for Bixby vision to extract the text.

It is one of the most practical uses of Bixby vision. To be able to store business card information and then store other contacts information within your phone.

Bixby Vision for translation

Bixby Vision can also translate words inside of the main wall, road sign, business card and kinds of stuff like that.

On the bottom left-hand corner, you have the translate logo

just tap on it, on the screen you have Auto-English.

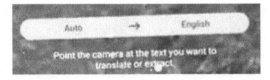

You can mainly go on and assign the language you want it to translate from. Place the phone on the text written on the object to translate while Bixby vision is on. Within a couple of seconds, it will translate the text on the object.

It is super practical and sees you using it to get you around, especially when you travel abroad, and you don't speak the language of the country.

Locate your location with Bixby vision

This feature can also help to pinpoint the location of a particular area, most notably when one is lost.

To use this feature, all you need is go to right-hand corner and tap on the location logo and point your phone straight down, and it is going to give you your location. There are also scan landmark to identify where you are.

Isn't the most practical things as you can pull up google map and that is going to pinpoint your location and probably more accurate than this, but it is still cool.

Control your camera with Bixby

You can also use Bixby to control your camera. The very first thing is to open your Bixby app, or you press and hold the side key if you have mapped it with the key. If you don't know how to get this done, endeavour to check the previous chapter.

Let's go through these examples.

Hey Bixby, "open the camera and take a picture with the rear camera."

It will take a picture with the rear camera.

Hey Bixby, "take a picture with the front camera."

It will get it done for you.

Hey Bixby, "start a video with the rear camera."

It will start recording the video using the rear camera just over my voice.

Hey Bixby, "take a live focus photo with the front camera."
I found this cool. You can pop your phone and put it on a tripod, and you control with your voice.

You can access Bixby vision in two different ways.
The first one is to open the camera and tap on the settings logo ⬛ at the left upper corner and is going to launch Bixby vision. The second one is using voice to open Bixby vision through this command "hey Bixby, open Bixby vision."

Chapter 16

5G supports

2020 marks a new direction for Samsung instead of focusing more on hardware and software. This year is all about creating a unique and outstanding experience. They believe 5G will be instrumental in making that happen.

All phones in the s20 line up have 5G supports, and for those who are technically inclined, the s20 supports sub six standard while the s20 plus and ultra support both sub six and millimetre-wave. Among the many benefits of 5G phones coupled with Aquarius that supports it is faster speed while streaming mobo games and at launch, Samsung is teaming with Microsoft to bring Forza street to the mobo platform. The game will be available for pre-order from Galaxy store very soon.

Chapter 17

Video & audio enhancement

Video and audio experience has to do with the best experience when you are watching movies or listening to music or watching videos on youtube.

To set this up, the first thing you have to do is go to settings then to advanced features and scroll all away down to video enhancer and enable it. It enhances the video quality to enjoy brighter and more vivid colours. Supported apps are seen below, and as you download more, it will reflect.

The other thing you are going to do to make sure you get the best experience is to scroll up and go to sounds and vibrations, all away down to sounds quality and effects then make sure DOLBY ATMOS sound is enabled. You can pick from the following options to change the sound effects.

- Auto
- Movie
- Music
- Voice

You can also manipulate these options from the notifications

panel all you have to do to hold on this logo . When you tap on the logo, toggles to enable and disable function, but if you tap on the text, it will get to quick button option. For the movie, hold the Dolby atmos logo, and it will show the quick button options for the movie.

163

Chapter 18

SIX essential applications

If you are new to android and especially the Samsung, there are five essential apps from Samsung that you must install on your new galaxy s20 series. These apps will just make your phone a lot easy and fun to use.

Video library

Let's talk about the first one. So in your gallery, you may have a mix of photos and videos, and you know the galaxy s20 series contains great videos. Still, there is no way to segregate them fairly; they are all mixed, and there is no sort of filter or sorting available for you to just look at videos.

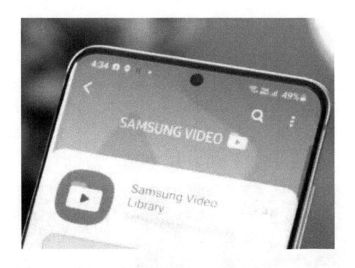

If you go to your Samsung galaxy store, not the play store and search for video library, you will get this app from Samsung once you installed it you will be able to then see only videos in respective folders in your galleries. The photos are not visible anymore, just videos making see them in different views. And the best part is that it plays videos instantly and right upfront. Of course, you can change the orientation, you can switch to full-screen mode if you still want to see your dark area, but I think it is a great tool to just look at videos.

One Hand Operation+

You can set up your s20 series side gestures to go back but if you long swipe you get all your controls, but if you long swipe diagonally down you will get your recent apps so you can quickly access them. You can swipe up diagonally to take a screenshot, or you can do the same on the Right Hand to go to your previous app. All of these are happening through this application called **One Hand Operation+**. You can configure the right edge and the left edge to perform certain activities which you generally do a lot of, and they are all just swiped away. Now you can configure one of this action so you know what it straight right to do what a diagonal up and a diagonal down should do and all of these options are available for you depending on what you are used to most you can configure.

Let's take long swipe as an example.

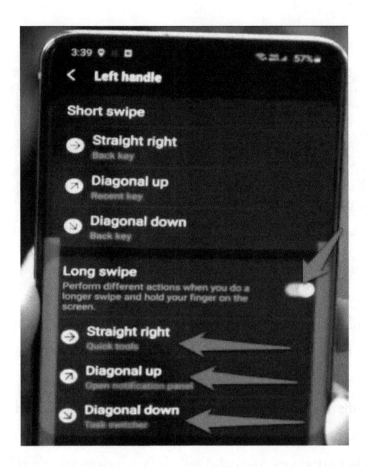

The first thing you have to do is to enable long swipe, and the swipe options will display underneath log swipe options. The swipe options are as follows;

- ❖ Straight right
- ❖ Diagonal up
- ❖ Diagonal down

If you swipe straight right, there are six options for you in which you can select for the action to perform. This method applies to other options in the application.

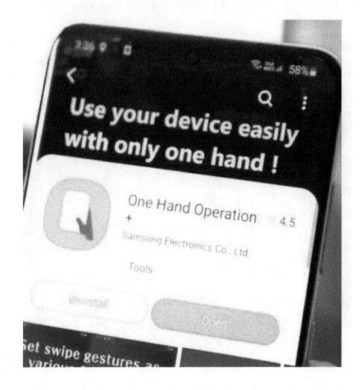

This application is available on the galaxy store and not the play store.

Samsung Email

Now the third one, funnily enough, Samsung doesn't include it need of Samsung email when the phone ships out to you.

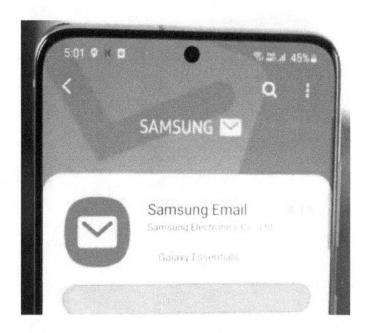

Now go to the galaxy store and download the Samsung Email app it's one of the email clients that's been used out there. Though you might have Gmail app, but if you are looking for something more official like a professional email application, then Samsung email is a must. It's free and full of features. For example, if you change the phone

orientation and you open the application, all messages will be displayed in the landscape.

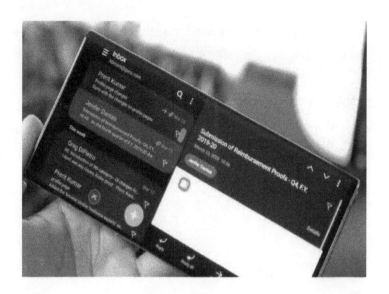

You will have a list style of view on the left and the reading pin on the left just like you have it on your desktop and also you can resize the window depending on what you need more of.

The inbuilt search functionality is one of the best have ever seen.

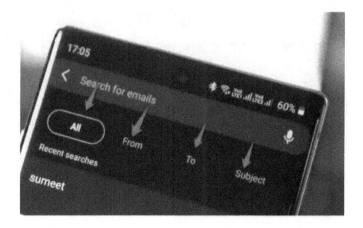

You can do your search just the way you do on the desktop.

You can search by all, from, to and the subject line that makes it a lot easier to look for the email.

If you want to write your email, there are a couple of formats and options such as; **list, indentation, bullets, bold, italics and all of that** are available which a lot of other email clients do not provide.

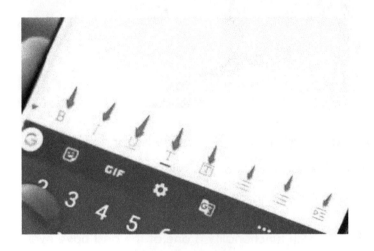

Edge Lighting+

Your galaxy s20 series comes about 607 Edge Lighting style, but this application has got fluid, boomerang and about 6 to 7 more that you probably do not have in your Edge Lighting effect.

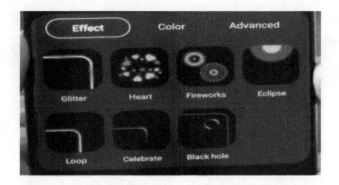

The effects are very cool. You can also set the transparency, width and the duration of your Edge Lighting. Go ahead to galaxy store and search for Edge Lighting+

Sound Assistant

Now you probably have a much boring looking volume control panel than the one in the image below.

The equalizer settings can be changed without really going into detailed sound settings, and you can also load any preset settings you have configured. So, all of these are happening right through this app called **Sound Assistant.** You can configure your volume control panel, and you can also change the color theme of the volume control panel which is pretty cool.

There are also a couple of other settings and for example, you can set individual app volume so every time you open apps, you can preset the volume it should play at which I think it's great flexibility to have. Also, you can have multi sounds which means multiple apps

174

together can play music and not just one specific app, which is the default from your system. It also enables us to have separate app sounds, for example,

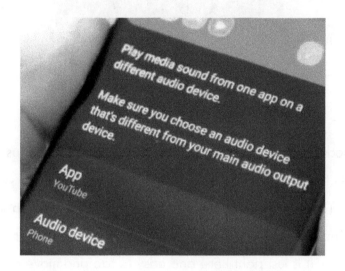

one app to play music in your earphone while another app can play through the phones speaker system, which again is very cool. To get this app, go to the galaxy store or play store and look for sound assistant and you will get this app.

Car mode

Car mode restricts the number of apps that you can use and changes the layout, so it's easier for you to use call while you are driving. You can increase the size of everything, so it's easier for you to tap. You don't have to be accurate, trying to focus more on the screen. It is just right here and easy to tap and move on.

Now, a couple of things you can do is; first, you can restrict the notifications that come from application, and you can decide which apps and block incoming calls altogether. You can also re-arrange the apps that you have isn't that a big deal. If you use the phone in landscape mode, you can select the navigation bar position. It depends whether you are driving on the left-side or right-side. The car mode automatically turns ON as soon as it detects you have connected to your car Bluetooth. The car mode automatically saves your parking location as early as you exit.

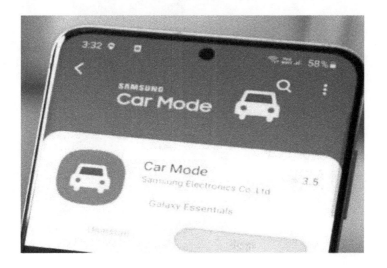

Overall, I think it is a pretty useful app if you use your phone a lot for driving purpose go ahead and download from the galaxy store.

So, these are the six essential Samsung galaxy apps for your s20 series, and I think they are beneficial for you.

Chapter 19

How to optimize battery life

- **Enable dark mode:** The s20 series featured AMOLED display which consumes battery dues to its functionality. Enabling dark mode reduces battery consumption than the regular light mode.

  The dark mode can be schedule base on when you need it. Under this, you can also disable adaptive brightness.

- **Activate standard refresh rate:** As you know, high refresh rate facilitates the battery consumption, and it gives more realistic animation and smoother scrolling. The standard refresh rate lasts longer the battery.

- **Reduce screen resolution:** This device supports quad display, but the 120Hz refresh rate is only supported on FHD+. HD+ and FHD+ will reduce battery consumption.

- **Reduce screen timeout:** You can reduce the screen timeout to about 30 seconds to enhance battery life.

- **Disable Edge lightning/reduce apps support:** Whenever a notification comes up, there is a colourful light around the edge of the screen. You can disable edge lightning or minimise the number of apps to support this feature in other to reduce battery consumption.

- **Activate maximum power saving:** If you like playing games, obviously you will go for high performance, but the best option for the regular use is the optimized mode and minimum power-saving mode. But if you want extreme battery saving, you can go with the maximum power-saving mode. You can also enable adaptive power saving mode to set the power mode automatically based on your usage pattern.

- **Activate adaptive battery:** This will limit battery for apps you don't use.

- **Disable always-on display:** Always-on display allows the screen to sleep in a daydream. Notifications, clock and date will be displayed when the screen is lock. Disable this to enjoy your battery life. This feature can also be scheduled.

- **Disable Samsung daily:** swipe your home screen to the right, toggle off to disable Samsung daily.

www.ingramcontent.com/pod-product-compliance
Lightning Source LLC
LaVergne TN
LVHW041211050326
832903LV00021B/571